RIDDLE FIELD

Riddle Field

Poems

Derek Thomas Dew

UNIVERSITY OF NEVADA PRESS | *Reno & Las Vegas*

University of Nevada Press, Reno, Nevada 89557 USA
www.unpress.nevada.edu

LIBRARY OF CONGRESS CATALOGING-IN-PUBLICATION DATA
Names: Dew, Derek Thomas, 1984– author.
Title: Riddle field : poems / Derek Thomas Dew.
Description: Reno ; Las Vegas : University of Nevada Press, [2020] |
Summary: "Riddle Field addresses the process of self-awareness and recovery in the
   wake of sexual trauma. In blending the voices of a fictional town about to be changed
   by the destruction of a dam, the book's poems highlight the environment from which
   trauma is born and kept secret" –Provided by publisher.
Identifiers: LCCN 2020017709 (print) | LCCN 2020017710 (ebook) |
ISBN 9781948908764 (paperback) | ISBN 9781948908771 (ebook)
Subjects: LCSH: Psychic trauma—Poetry. | LCGFT: Poetry.
Classification: LCC PS3604.E893 R53 2020 (print) | LCC PS3604.E893
   (ebook) | DDC 811/.6—dc23
LC record available at https://lccn.loc.gov/2020017709
LC ebook record available at https://lccn.loc.gov/2020017710

The paper used in this book is a recycled stock made from 30 percent post-consumer
waste materials, certified by FSC, and meets the requirements of American National
Standard for Information Sciences—Permanence of Paper for Printed Library Materials,
ANSI/NISO Z39.48-1992 (R2002). Binding materials were selected for strength and
durability.

FIRST PRINTING

24 23 22 21 20   5 4 3 2 1

Manufactured in the United States of America

For Michelle

Achilles: "Grief of the people" Untouchable

Bishōnen: "Beautiful youth (boy)." A young man whose beauty and sexual appeal transcend the boundary of gender or sexual orientation.

Contents

V.

Acknowledgments

"Mainland," "Winchuck," and "Old Carver"
appeared in *Two Hawks Quarterly.*

"Confluence," "Liar's Dice," and "He Ring"
appeared in *The Maynard.*

"Reliquary 1," "Reliquary 2," "Reliquary 3," "Reliquary 4"
appeared in *Interim.*

Special thanks to: Arthur Vogelsang, Jami Macarty,
The Maynard, Elena Karina Byrne, Rusty Morrison,
Two Hawks Quarterly

I

Town in the Radio

When it's cold and wet, more is revealed:
    Autumnboy, I stood naked in front of a man.

The music everybody knows from the radio
    defends the empty highway.

The moss of a city back east
    draws into the pores of its red brick.
Miscast.

Death is the bookmark fallen to the floor.
    An America of stages, of bartenders,

of assassins learning to dance feeds my hand,
    which despite my attempts will not become

the colored glass of taverns now that I am a man.
    Moss is music proves all rain tastes the same.

Crude meaning good, crude meaning innocent,
    the singer has all the hair ripped off her upper lip,
an American smile never forced.
    I pick myself up off the ground again.

I can't fit into the man's book.
    I'm a town in the radio.

Wind is to pray the heavyset woman
    doesn't fall from her bicycle.

Mainland

She'll cut off all her hair the day they blow the dam.

The boy at church told her some trees don't collect water with their roots.

At midnight in the canyon she was in her little bra trying to dance for him.

Before they could kiss, a cow went into labor and screamed, and the boy ran.

A dam of cattails. A dam ten thousand feet high.

Swim like a baby, he said. It will be a holiday.

All the boy has done will be the bottom of a lake in the V of his arms.

First, there was only the candle's flame crawling the bathwater.

Then, traveling the rim of the tub, a light like the one atop his jeep.

It's really just a big wall and when we finish it, we'll be given a new shirt.

Far from Walter

The girl I like discovers the blueprint for every hall is a crack in stone.
Pageantry. Herringbone. Blind till them fall.
Water on the duck path from Fauntleroy to the darlingtonias.
Here is far from Walter who doesn't limp.
FM guitars cut the steam rising off the freshly seeded lily field.
One day you'll come to your senses and realize, without a stick,
you'd limp.
After they blow the dam, you shuffle your silks, elsewhere run the
foxes.
If a ball left in the field is indecisive, then is an O indecisive as well?
A carbide lamp is always exploding. Foxes run the length of it.
The prisoner need only speak, but it's an errand dismantled by
a name.

Wet Down

Without enough rain, the river pulls salt from the harbor.
  The end of all portraits, now you've heard cat, bird, flood.
As through a choir light between the bowstring and brotherly hand.
  You don't wet down the box elder, it cracks, and that's food off
    the table.
Air through dead river cane draws kin, the turkeys muted and
  forgiven.
  The one that was counting something about me lives on a glacier.
Oars into soil and a ripple-portrait above the hearth. Said this to me:
  You must first be known to my voice if my voice is to be known
    to you.
A radiant green aching crossbar. We keep our turkeys in a burned-out
  redwood.
  Weapons we weapons, no one who took the oath believes in
    the drought.

Old Carver

Hog lard and turpentine for the mosquitoes plus others for the smell.
I've hated that creek since I was three apples high. It's incapable.
Suspension bridges, fourth century. Every mountain wants to be flat.
The bones of her bird may kick into dance when it floods.
Out of the unworlding peatblack dripstone, you would think a
hammer, but
In our case nobody would slow down or look at us. An inch a year.
Bred for it: a piece of corn on the cob abandoned on the railroad tracks.
The spring wants the steepest, weakest of shingle, vowel.
A crater has no suffix. In a single syllable, it bullfrogs black out of black.
*A twig of bird spine pricks the soft sill bottom, and names bud
across our throats.*

Confluence

A dusty grand piano falls out a two-story window into a water fountain
　below.
　My father threw orange peels at coyotes in the dusk.
Red rocks. Mast passes slow behind shafts of river cane.
　Walter, the first time you scratched my shoulder the desert
where the rock swallows the river. Roman candle headlight.
　A chimney for the first time. Letters in erupting kilns.
The man walking the valley knows the pickaxe nightpale music.
　They fought Apache for that hill so we could live and perfume the
　　doorways.
They probably don't have a word for *piano* in their language anyway.
　Little orange peels are not meteors. They dry like armies into
　　hymns.

Yellow Corner

Now the barber in the yellow corner has drunk just enough to close up
early.

Oils from your finger will kill this cave's wall, you can see it there.

But we must know a place through the exclusions of the human word.

Why it is we never feel the splitting of a glacier when k is.

Now the nurses stop to buy coffee from a laundromat on their walk
home.

*And if the hill is still blue smoke when the snow climbs to counters,
we'll surely freeze.*

You'll seal it. Nothing will grow again. One touch.

*Torn brown from the vinegar. Porch is chipping. Red lips held up
by a coat rack.*

The word has flooded this cave, yet this cave is not flooded.

*Saying "counters and counters and counters" keeps the snow
down.*

The Nameless

All the arrows painted on the road contain microabrasions.

Someone threw a Spanish guitar at the sheriff's windshield.

The calf's hoof splits sandstone as it clamors to life.

Peter drew a pair of knives on the door to the dead strip club.

Even the tiniest breath arranges the mountains and stills the waters.

It was so dim that the red flowers on the carpet seemed to glow.

A calf's face has a canyon's sense of symmetry.

A brown tooth rattles in an empty beer bottle atop its head.

The plow tears the street up along with the snow.

There's a Spanish guitar painted on the bus rolling out of town.

Winchuck

I heard a sound in the night–they were slicing up the life raft.

   *In the morning I saw the horses had left the field for the winter. At
      the gas station they*

                                                                    knew

The men are still up on the hill talking about when the lake goes, so
   will the money.

   *I bought the girl I like a frog, but I only see her when she comes to
      the gas station.*

And the wind shortens the cliff, but there can be no acronym for it.
   Consequent roadside tree.

   *All our iron nowadays comes from melted-down refrigerators and
      microwaves.*

A deer-cry shelter in the yellow above allnight, forgotten ore in the
   stream.

   *A life raft endless in the fiddleheads and plum sod. Peter drew
      knives*

Like the druid takes the wild boar's name.

   Our words, the town's, are kite-dead bees exiting a hawk.

I'm Walter

Some stretch their legs out and place their feet far to claim domain.
Some keep their legs together and their knees half-topple to one side.
Some cross their legs and are not unpleasant to speak with.

I've made towns of fathers out of small afraid boys
who peel the stickers off my model helicopters
while my force has no beginning and no end,
an action that has always been a memory
like an average man in a town.

I had wanted to give
if not mine when was he
of my little intensities
a now I never know
what in the flesh I had wanted
to share until broken like flesh
a fever tans his wrist
rich in dead yawn of a trash truck
moaning through an alley
on the last day of California.

Baby Prince

Cenotaph, cavitation. The druid mimics the wild boar.

If a baby prince, I only have two shovels.

Cade lamb in undulations–we destroy our signifiers.

A hill shortens a root, we shorten a hill.

Stepping on one foot heavier, you end up walking in circles.

Annie gypsy Annie Annie at the top of the flood.

Flakes of usnea thatching swim at the boar's hoof.

A prince's shirt pouring from the lamb's neck.

His kingdom ain't empty, my dad says, his kingdom ain't empty.

The druids loved each other's bodies in the sands of summer battle.

Articles

The café isn't much. I was born at the only booth in the window.

The people are gonna be here about those bones. Scientists and like that.

My bike makes the café look bigger than it is. Rivers are like teased sheets.

I heard that raccoons got bones in their dicks. Is that like us?

Walter came to the gas station, and said girls don't like me.

Nobody cared until the bones belonged to some lost thing. Am I of name?

Behind the café they've roped off several areas of interest.

I wet the girl I like's new frog every few minutes with a rag. She'll be here, I think.

Walter never visits the café. You can't buy cigarettes, and he hates the girls.

Studying the smoke's failed accent across his face—did you go away or did I?

He Ring

Each bird a canal into the dam, when it blows, a little two-step, a bird
    porcelain stride.
    Model helicopters, mother buried deep in the model helicopters.
A bicycle with a good escape, laughing all the time, never laughing.
    He doesn't mind if I flush the toilet and pee into it while it goes
       down.
By saying Walter, you have unsaid Walter, yet all berries are meant for
    Walter.
    An axe golden black in the charcoal sketch, the freedom to make
       prisoners.
Brushing his teeth at the river.
    I am not so chosen for freedom, but from freedom. Bereaved of
       hatchet.
Why not always the orange door, I am slow, I remember thinking.
    Fighter, I am thinking, he is the ring. Walter is where I do my
       fighting.

Grin Burnt

A name written in glitter glue on a folded card on a desk, mine.
  *A century's meaning, particulars of a baseball diamond without
    a crowd.*
Low fog cow swabbed. Bike known. A road my father never yawned.
  *It took nine dogs to fill the main road when they swept for
    homeless.*
The cops took portrait after portrait. You think the portraits are under
  the water?
  Corrugated tines of white shoulder grin burnt. Afraid to look up.
Home plate under lights, pollen to the spring landing, cold pavement
  thighs.
  *Little knit goat, am I part of a trilogy? My dad's garage is doomed,
    I'm afraid.*
The name on the folded card on the desk, white phones pearling
  earlobes.
  *Nine dogs, a chin as grey. We're made of score and pottery dust
    deep.*

Little Bread

A household in flames crawls through a horse, the horse in the
foreground.
*Walter The Much Too Tall says each man decides the boundaries
of his town.*
He offered me coffee. Was the town old enough for coffee?
*The cook at the café paid for the girl I like's bus fare. He said she's
crooked or lucky.*
Everything is a dam: an unself in the white dive who becomes a king
lost in his own town.
*Trace canyons. Learn, lover, learn. His hand was as trustworthy as
steam from the mill.*
The torch of his chest a gaze with many aisles. Smoke is song and
ceiling.
The cook at the café said our beers are on the demolition guys.
A house crawls into boy, the name. (Walter takes me in hand.)
I stood quiet at the door. A yawn from the little bread.

Last November's Burn

For granddad's funeral, cousin Chris had a case of Newcastle and a
  bottle of Powers.
  The neighbor's cockatoo leaned every which way inside the
    neighbor's house.
Cousin Chris said he'd take the Buick apart with his fists if the bottle
  wasn't returned.
  The neighbor fell into his yard. He cried out to the fleeing
    cockatoo. The bird, all of it.
And then here comes Aunt Pam with this smoke like last November's
  burn.
  Cousin Chris said he was sorry for it, but he wasn't up for the hunt
    of no ill cockatoo.
The mama cow's back squeezed the Budweiser sign against the barn.
  The word boy, the name boy. Now I'm going to need liquor or I'm
    going to need seed.
I secretly gave the heifer calf to Osvaldo's hungry family and lied to
  my dad.
  Osvaldo has helped my dad for twenty years. His son's tin is too
    thin. I had to.

The Mermaid Club

They were giving out popcorn on the den's last day.

Little battleground mermaids painted on the side wall.

And watching my friend love my mother on the wall.

A tiny rogue hare, when everyone said son, you thought daughter.

Do I ask for grace? Some kind of cooing?

Walter wet Walter went an end to all portraits.

How is he made me feel indebted to show me my name.

When I was little I thought as the crow flies meant desire.

The whole town dried up like a payphone.

To end it, he rode into the mermaids painted on the side wall.

Soft Thieves

Get off your bike early and you'll have to bop your way back.
  You're getting your lanes confused, kid. Crime is lazy, it ain't
    stupid.
She told me that in French, *passion* takes more syllables.
  She told me the Beach Boys would never visit town or like my mom.
Wherever men met her, they took the lane to the mechanic's house.
  Formerly recovery, she now teaches about cracks in vases,
that a penny bike's wheel phrase can be warped and dusted.
  What work is work enough to pin a three-letter word on Walter?
All the boppers the day breaks into a pool chainlink.
  She walked across hot coals into the heart of the Beach Boys.

Blue Masking Tape

Shovel. Gavel. Soapbox. Not enough milk as a lad.

No more state-line market. All the car symbols are disappearing.

Each berry a summit verge, I called it World War Me.

Walter is any solid object that winds tiny hands, cotton pitsong.

Chris told me adamantium isn't real. I never asked Walter.

No more state-line market. Dam stuttering feather.

Toll posture overnight. Church-sized mirror.

My kept-small hand, blue-masking-tape-clasped wedding ring.

Perishables on shelf, dam stuttering both roofs.

Flood halting all archives: shovel, gavel, Shoebox, Ford.

Gambit

The cock droops,
the linoleum shines;

the moon outside, an unknowing,
finds its coin in the brow of a riverbank before

leaving the field to its corn;
the white-skinned boy sinks before a rusty gate,

the gate rattles off a crow; a young mother circles
a cracked driveway, dried shards of stem

and pinched arnica in her feet; the wind ties clouds
to sand with a common lash; after being zipped back up

the boy is in bed and hears a jet cross the sky so
distance is men standing and talking where men have died;

somebody learns to crave this offense like the sting of ice;
clumps of fern feed black trees which are where one looks

when wishing to look at nothing;
the river traps the dead

in a brick lip; a man's room is balsam smoke silking
past flakes of green bud caught in black tassels

hanging from the high table
and charred horseflies in the mouths of candles

promise to draw breath
is to find the choir in stone.

Big Drown

He spent countless nights trying to draw a perfectly straight line.
> *But I was told that you cannot petition the lord with prayer.*

The ceramic cub is the safety. Jackson presented the Tiffany.
> *A man gets older, he doesn't like killing. Better off hauling silver out of Nevada.*

Dad used Camel cash to get me a trench lighter. Ervol Gavel, a name.
> *Simplicity is one thing. A man can live in simplicity. But to say it is another thing.*

Ervol Gavel, a cigarettes jacket to school, and school took my Joe Camel jacket.
> *The maple of Conn. The ash of Penn. The red birch of NH. And the oak of NY state.*

Ervol Gavel is called a father or a man? The adults argue.
> *At the historical society they theorize about what was vermilion from Kentucky.*

Inosculation

If any one of us eats alone, he becomes a child.

The dust devils return sweep the face off the Elk's Club.

In the belfry a girl strikes a match on the butcher's window.

From up there the cheese wheels button across the glass.

Bevy of bucks too young to climax. A signature. An ink.

Children know to grip their sleeves when putting on their jackets.

Blindspeed charcoal and laurel and you think belfry cowards.

If one of us becomes a child, then all of us become children.

Charcoaled bell collared with jousting Roosevelts.

Like a name in sign language, it's a kind of grafting onto silence.

Short Leg

The old calendar has gone proud. You've been interpreted?

    To a child a flood is losing sight of a flying bird.

She left a gun in Milwaukee and never looked older than in the music.

    To a child, a flood is losing sight of a flying bird.

The smell of Tabu before school and lipstick on a tissue in the toilet.

    To a child, a flood is losing sight of a flying bird.

The guys at the pawn shop don't want her old jewelry but take a
menthol.

    To a flood, a sight of losing child is a flying bird.

With a mask on, not every portrait is deaf. I never get used to his
knock.

    To a child, a flood is losing sight of a flying bird.

Border Huts

When my mother and I would split pole, she'd say bread and butter.

By now, the army must be when the drummer leaves himself.

Chris says it actually snowed in town back then in the Thirties.

In the end, I'm so angry because my hands are too small.

Give you the last, give you Ervol on the cymbal at the border huts.

Can't punch right or hold a drumstick in the proper fashion.

By now, there is a twenty-four-hour drummer made of thousands of
movies.

For Chris, in all of the boulevard clocks the night was in the digging.

The movies where they say things like back after sundown no later.

*So that he might look back, and be thrilled at a younger man's
appetite.*

Low Bite

The dam won't wait for the young convict who makes bread at the
    diner.
    Walter told me the band on the Titanic played while sinking to
        the end.
He approaches with a little green knife tattooed on each of his hands.
    Smoke adorned with a terrace through the bandstand, encoded,
        ulterior.
A pouring of gorgeous sourdough that found plate but wouldn't melt
    butter.
    Their last song was "Nearer My God to Thee," styled either Yank
        or Brit.
A garlic shard the size of a tooth keystones pearl and plane.
    Each fault in the ship a long bald arch running ice through suncut
        throat.
The bread is undercooked but the guests smile and compliment it.
    Peatblack ankles freeze inchmeal.

From Trains

Noon sun through a pearl. We didn't want to start naming movies.
  Me and the girl I like tried to sneak into the drive-in. The rain and
    hoist down to heist.
The young convict who makes bread at the diner loaned me his
  Murray's hair stuff.
  They took Ervol's Zippo and kicked us out even though I told them
    Ervol was my pop.
The young convict pressed his cat's cheeks against his warm coffee
  mug. Firmament

                                              Roosevelt scarf.
  Me and the girl I like saw the cooks tossing a basketball on
    our way to the bus station.
She said they reminded her of tree stumps or phone booths led from
  the trains to the

                                                        drive-in.
  We found a Poppy Ott book on a bench and took turns reading
    the poems fans had

                                                    mailed in.
Scoop Ellery and I are chums, says the young George Butler at 819
  North State St.,

                                              Jackson, Miss.
  We kissed laughing as Ralph Mohat, 538 Prospect St., Marion,
    Ohio, says Bid shoves

                                      Jerry into a gutter.

My Helicopters

Only gabachos and donkeys walk in the noonday sun.

Today they were closing up the secondhand store for good.

In the movie the boy recites times tables while the young man

Some women film their child's birth, Walter said women should be clay.

crouches in the reeds and evens out a crooked spear shaft with his teeth.

The mannequin in the abandoned secondhand store, what did you tell it?

I told it that it looks like my Aunt Avery who has curves like Adrienne Barbeau.

If you're going to help me build one of my helicopters you have to keep secrets.

What I really told it was that it looks like my mom who has curves like a school bus.

And then Walter showed me a picture of two rifle bullets that had collided in midair.

Light Us Down

All earth in a broken comb before the batting cages.

Chris says we crave motion out of fear and that's why the dam's going.

My aunt was here before the dam, fixing people's fountains and mowing lawns.

Bounced out of bingo—a heartshot, it was within the hierarchies.

The Yanks and Brits hear the same song, each think it's their country's version.

Fellow cattlemen accordion flourish like a spider through the butt of a bottle.

My aunt was here digging into the limestone before the batting cages.

Will my Zippo work, will there be a band playing when they blow the dam?

Robbing the bingo game to bedrock, she died a fake name in an old book.

At the batting cages, my aunt breathed the pitch that killed the girl I like.

That Clapping

What if you were surrounded by water, how'd that be?

   Maybe the Beach Boys knew we crave motion out of fear.

The young convict put a newt under his baseball cap.

   A cave says once long ago there were no surnames.

You'll know water's reach when you know who is last to run and who
   is last to serve.

   The gardener might be a good pitcher, but he's got it all wrong.

     Born is let off the

                                        leash.

If you discuss someone else's face long enough it will begin to
   resemble your own.

   Blessed are those allowed. Allowed to bring you beauty. You're
     never deserving, only

                                   allowed.

You ever eaten eggs and toast that made you feel like you been
   around for centuries?

   In the gardener's cigar, their clapping is a slow beach.

Cat Root

I guess the big thing is that my jacket might smell like his.

*Me and Osvaldo's son crawled under the boardwalk and scared
  people walking above.*

I wanted to loiter, but I was a name without a sound and a cat was on
  a fence as I ran by.

*Recarved by the unlikely orange of a single headlight, my hands
  have stayed five years*

old.

A burnt beach doesn't benefit from a flood. Death is only a cat on a
  fence as I run by.

*A woman wearing a skirt passes over, and I notice that Osvaldo's
  son is looking at me.*

(A stolen forty-oz. in the spilling coins if the desert thigh was such that
  you'd die to let it happen.

*Foxgloves split the drummer flesh: My little mansion, in a skinning
  class.*)

Osvaldo's son runs his fingers up and through the fern at the bottom
  of the stairs.

Gray-perfect chin and arms of the jacket now horns on the couch.

Ring Up Dawn

How can I use the word <u>and</u> if I have to wrap masking tape around my
    wedding ring?
If I touch the dam, will it die like a cave or will a fault line appear
    signaling a new cave?
Moon over welder is an ageless corner rivet. Soon, we'll need boats.
Given to the hope of wildfire, an oarsman in the birch scoops a
    kid from a floating roof.
Something in the way he never asked me to forgive him his discordant
    tone.
By dawn the welder is finished although unsure of what he has
    accomplished.
A warbling snare sounds for each wave like a tongue underarm.
From a distance, the name written on the dam looks like a crack.
The oarsman is crow's feet across a candlewick. Last to run.
One glove catches another as if in the beginning, I was a stranger
    to myself.

IV

Griddle Six

I found a table and chairs caught inside a girl
caught inside cold sun.

Stray dogs are cop cars like wasps taking root in a hair salon.
A bottle cap lodged in asphalt is its own limousine.

Her age is in her neck; she mimics the snore of the oldest
woman at the bus station.

White every third mountain is a tooth am I as old
as the fathers in movies?

I've said yes someone to someone lost to road in a tan line.

My compass is a boy who needs a compass
as well as to get the cheese to griddle six.

The biggest embarrassment to royalty is rain.
The way you describe a door indicates if you'd open it.

Liar's Dice

My hands are under the roots under the trees, and the trees are under
the lake.

*Walter, the flood, made me swear not to snitch on him if my mom
found the magazine.*

And animals and rope burn are one animal. Face redder in each bee-
dipped finger.

*I am digging into the dam with my bare hands. I get a letter for
the guy here before me.*

When they blow the dam, will the river meet the sea? The river stays
apart from the sea.

*I am not a bobtail. Walter gave me a name with no sound. I am
elbow-deep in the dam.*

My aperture: he said he'd make a diamond of my magazine-crowded
mouth.

*As chosen as a photo, as familiar to a harbor as a neighbor with
no shoes.*

Walter lost a calf playing liar's dice.

*It was sand in the dam. Sand that trapped my fingers. Sand that
traced the equator.*

Tunnel Music

I can know my hand only as my own.

Had I been speaking in a language born in me, yet foreign to me?

I will never look at it and see my father's hand.

*Was mine a language whose echo searched me but found no
    father?*

I will never look at it and see my mother's hand.

*Did Walter, the flood, give me my true tongue when even my
    mother would lie to me?*

I know my hand only as a man knows a fence he's painting.

Was it I who forced it down under the roots under the trees?

Years pass over my hand; my father had no brothers.

I found a page with my portrait in his magazine.

Watchcoat

On the edge of Osvaldo's ranch there's a little wooden tollbooth.
> *If I run there and stand in it, and shut the door, will the flood never reach me?*

Lying upside down in Ervol's truck, it looks like a flute coming down from heaven.
> *Might it cut that final deep like a watchcoat, breach the surface, and burst into flames?*

I would gladly burn my shirt; a countryside dies for lack of a lamp.
> *In need of a windlass, "one continuous jaw"–black night, burning ship.*

A waitress at the café says there's a lake on top of a mountain where shipwrecks pop up.
> *How many little shapes do you need to be? A single tollbooth should be sufficient.*

Orange peels ride the chop on the surface of a water a hundred calves deep.
> *Soon, the first light, and I notice I'm sewn into my clothes.*

Ducksing

A boy can fear his street or he can fear his father, he can never fear
both.

Being such a mutiny that no mutiny would follow, Osvaldo made a
tent out of his cow.

The owner of the café interviewed me about being a dishwasher. He
asked me about

Ervol.

Osvaldo put buckshot in its head, then went looking for half-
smoked cigarettes on the

train tracks.

I couldn't answer the questions about Ervol, but the owner answered
them himself after

asking.

Osvaldo propped the cow up on three rusty pieces of rebar and
sliced it up the belly.

I saw Ervol on the train tracks after dark and thought he was a
homeless man, so I ran.

The cow was opened at dusk. Osvaldo's son found him sleeping
under it the next

morning.

To fear your father is to "feed upon the creature that feeds your lamp."

Osvaldo refused to come out from under his cow, he would only
repeat the word

punctilio.

Placeholder

The mirror opened my brow, but I had napkins from the café.

The dusk is an army without a drummer in the little tollbooth.

Blue masking tape holds the mirror together.

The tollbooth like a boy finding the street in his father's face.

The mermaids came off the wall to drink from the dam's cracks.

The body of a virgin eats the trees from the ground up.

Every tollbooth's vow in splinters across the mermaids' breasts.

A boy shaves his head; a virgin enters a tree and tries to drink.

All silences kept are not kept in silence.

The mermaids are washed away before reaching the tollbooth.

Trouble Knuckle

I sat in the tollbooth with stolen wine and a sister living inside my
hands.
*The Roosevelts across the road huddled like the melted trunk of
a candle.*
Afraid to look up. Does a building besiege its own ash? Afraid to look
up.
*The last of the town's pageantry is draped around the Roosevelts'
necks.*
I pushed the cork down into the bottle so it sloshed like a building in
a flood.
*The sister inside my hands traced canyons in the planks of soft
wood.*
A duckpath cut the reeds and the streetlights became drinking straws.
*You must first be known to my voice if my voice is to be known
to you.*
If it's Dad, he won't make me stop climbing the building.
Could it be that an entire sentence was crafted out of my name?

Elkstone

Squeezing an accordion won't shake the father from the photo.

It was a Roosevelt, but once inside the crosshairs it was a branch.

Once inside a photo, a hammer can only make suggestions.

What else tortures you like asylum for your servant?

It was a shelter, but once in the crosshairs, it was a man.

I watched the man play the accordion outside the laundromat.

What servant knows to keep an urn filled with his master?

A flood will allow only its own music to weave through antlers.

Wood or stone should occupy a man's hands.

See, I don't trust no Christ that don't stay on the cross.

The Allowance

The hammer in the photo looks like a boxcar in a plum.
  I no longer need any seed nor chicken wire.
The hammer in the photo is a whalebone corset.
  I no longer need the cows, nor their rhyming prayer.
The hammer in the photo is an owl atop a cairn.
  I no longer need the dust of the spent baseball field.
The hammer in the photo is a foxglove out of season.
  I no longer need grace, nor any manner of cooing.
The hammer in the photo is a spoke dry of all wine.
  The flood has come, and I'm able to see the islands.

Cairn

Ruins of the video store peek above the water.

I know that under the flood, the islands are connected.

All the Christ on film trapped at the bottom of a lake.

If ever there was a Second Coming, it would end our hope.

The other movies, the dirty ones, might have a prayer.

A mother dying in childbirth is the only sacrifice not regretted.

The dirty ones are sealed in the oil from a great number of hands.

I grin at thee, thou grinning whale.

Humans live on human hope; the dirty movies burn now and always.

I will never forget that under the flood, the islands are connected.

Topples Cake

The fake whales kept sinking when they went to film *Moby Dick.*
> *Your head is good if your hand makes you dizzier than the older boys' stories.*

The fake whales nestle in the sand out front of the submerged bowling alley.
> *I use my hand to think about the women painted on the wall of the Mermaid Club.*

Talk English to a fake whale, and it'll feel stupid. Talk gibberish, and you meet it halfway.
> *A chimney flooded from the top.*

The sea only makes sea.
> *Your hand is good if it topples cake.*

Somebody must portage the fake whale.
> *After Walter, I think with my hands.*

V̄

Between Churches

The theater once made music for loquats.
Every balcony spilled into its own echo

like repetition is the nausea that brings clarity.
An usher boy sneaks into the bathroom right after

his favorite singer has been there just to smell her
uninterrupted.

Like repetition is the nausea that brings clarity,
the young woman who teaches senior water aerobics

has a miscarriage, with thirty elderly women watching
in the pool at the health club, the burgundy ribbon

mushrooming around their wrinkled knees
like a fight you were in but can't

remember the details of

the red water is octopi.

Land That Knows Hands

Some blithe quartz vein walks the skull. I say what's done is done.

The sun was a sandstone etching and my bike was tall until the flood.

Can you see these hands? Handlebars and cherries.

Do you choose to see these hands?

What's done isn't done. All these waters were made to recede.

He had me again thinking of Dad missing out on all the world wars.

I can use the word <u>and</u> but my fingers will not grow.

Many would see a blithe quartz vein as merely decoration.

What is a human heart but the living fury of a dead language?

Gladly, I lied, and said I was a woman.

Cursorial

Somewhere under it all, lie the Easter lilies.

    Maybe I'll be funny, because you can always trust funny.

The ones dislodged by the water now toes in a new museum.

    I put these socks on long ago; a princely nod to a rack of gowns.

I wandered through the empty state-line market with a cat at either
    door.

    And still I avoid looking at my country. In the pitch black, a cat
        bathes himself.

Now, I have nailed my doubloon to the mast, and skinned a whale
    cock for my robe.

    A row of trees with all but one tucked behind the fog. The
        neighbors are burning.

The Easter lilies swim through the state-line market. My doubloon
    waits in the clay.

    Day allowed no wet sand. Dusk revoked the bell. In harmony,
        I'm adapted for

                                      running.

Reliquary 1

Anything far away
is a lighthouse.
The opera singer
whom people only want
to hear hum
spots one
on the water
off in the distance.

It's actually the locksmith's roof
peeking above the flood,
but nobody has to know.

Later, he walks out to a balcony
–hears a loud crack–
and watches the calico horses
scatter through the trees.

Somewhere, on the side of the road,
there are bees in a hawk.

Reliquary 2

Don't bear anywhere because he may not
flood (hand) peanut & peasant.
Summer wants the weakest shingle.

I feel safer.
Walking the white fence.
Gather Gander Garden,
and the mermaids painted on the side wall.

With a mask on, not every portrait is deaf.

Reliquary 3

My wedding ring clinks
on the bottle I try to
sip from before opening.

A hawk rips the violin
that keeps the meadow.

Silver corn sheaf
asleep in a fist.

Long ago, me and my mother
had a happy first night
in a new apartment.
Soon after, I inherited
my sister's bedroom.

You can't draw a beach.

Honor
is to never sneeze

Reliquary 4

I painted a white line on the gravel
but the stones walked away.
As I went down the road, the old-timer
approaching the mailbox was whistling.
What a tune! I thought. And

though pierced by birdsong, it followed.
Before long I was at the docks, burning
laundry. But still this whistle followed.
Mice mossed a trumpet. Day came train
bending into the tunnel before connected I

two or three moths singing their small
hearts for the wet dusk and lights
flashing green. Down the road, it's
all this neon. But down the fence,
the same green whistle.

By now, we have laughed at either side
of the volcano. We touched the spot on
the owl where moon might have an ear.
I painted a white line across a whale
but didn't know a single man at sea.

Very

1.

Something lived in that refuses
to stay in me–a desert twilight
painted on an old van.

To boost young strength
a father fakes injury when he shakes his son's hand.

Very is lived in through likelihood only
or degree only.

When the son becomes a man, he studies the back of
another man's neck, keeping to himself what he discovers there.

By language we mean agreement,
like how every little clearing in the forest is a living room.
If there was a shout, it couldn't do.

The man's neck is every wrong name
for the bend of the train.

Now this is me
after his hand met my own.
Very was degree only.

Child gone unto skin gone of my stories.
A surface that moves
like a parlor travels.

2.

Rings clink together:
how odd to be a pregnant woman
in Louisiana just waking up.

Afterward

A child's bare back twitches
away from the cold back
of a chair:

The lines at the party have not met.
There is music, and there is nothing
behind the house.

Each crescendo like a man
taking a deep breath
as you pass by him in a car.

Notes

In "Baby Prince," the word *cenotaph* refers to a monument for a person who is buried elsewhere. "Cavitation" refers to the formation of an empty place inside a body or a solid object. *Cade* means domesticated. *Usnea* is the lichen one finds attached to limbs and bark on trees in the forest, particularly in the Pacific Northwest.

About the Author

Derek Thomas Dew's literary work has appeared in a number of anthologies, including *Dead and Undead Poems: Zombies, Ghosts, Vampires and Devils*, *Noble Dissent*, *Not a Drop*, *Elementary My Dear Watson*, and *The Bees' Breakfast*. His poetry has appeared in journals, including Interim, *Twyckenham Notes*, *The Maynard*, *The Curator*, *Two Hawks Quarterly*, and *Hawaii Pacific Review*. His manuscript "Almond Psalm" was a semi-finalist in American competitions for the Word Works Washington Prize, the Elixir Press Antivenom Award, and the Brittingham Prize. He is a winner of an Oregon Opportunity Grant and an Omnidawn Publishing Workshop Scholarship. His readings include international events at The Poets' House in Donegal, Ireland and at the Lancaster Poetry Festival in Lancaster, England. His work has been translated into Chinese and has been published in several Asian periodicals.